MW01205007

# TREIGN

# TREIGN

## Empowered to Discover

Unless otherwise indicated, all scripture quotations in the volume are from the English Standard version of the Bible.

First Printing 2021

ISBN 978-1-7378124-0-1

# CONTENTS

I dedicate this book to my wife Karen who has stood by me and believed God.

The book that you hold in your hand is one in series of teaching on reigning in life through the one man Jesus Christ.

"For if, because of one man's trespass, death reigned through that one man, much more will those who receive the abundance of grace and the free gift of righteousness reign in life through the one man Jesus Christ." Romans 5:17

## Introduction:

What if I told you that you have been duped into believing a lie about yourself? What if I showed you that the real reason for your existence has been concealed from you? What if I revealed to you that your life is so important that it has been conspired against, and that strategies, plots and plans have been devised to keep you from discovering your true uniqueness? What if I told you that your destiny is in plain sight, but the camouflage of this world has kept you from realizing it? Would you be surprised that this entire world system with all of its glory, accolades, information and wisdom is in direct opposition in regard to who you really are?

Humanity has been under siege by ancient forces seeking man's extermination. Mankind has been a slave through a sophisticated captivity that gives the appearance of freedom through sin and self-will but is in reality a shackled existence with severe constraints and limitations, detaining humankind from realization of true identity!

Regardless of your present station in life, you were created for so much more! You are an intricately detailed creation crafted to do something specifically significant in the time you are on earth!

Countless resources have been expended, and entities mobilized to keep you from hearing the truth. From the time of your birth until now, strategic plans, and a matrix of deception has been woven around you to keep you from discovering your true purpose, gifting and power!

The purpose of this book is to acquaint you with the truth about who you really are, reveal the way to your true identity and empower you to walk in its reality.

In these pages you will see that you have been **"Empowered to Discover!"** your purpose, your provision, and your power!

# Chapter One: Conspiracy Theories

Throughout the history of man there has been no shortage of conspiracy theories. From Roswell to secret government programs, to the agendas of secret societies, the ruminations of man are endless. However, the greatest conspiracy ever perpetrated on humanity is not a theory, but a harsh reality. The greatest hoax ever to be played on humanity is the concealing of their true identity! Mankind has been sold into a system that is counter intuitive to their original design. The function of man is perverted, causing him to not function right. A virus has altered man and caused him to live well below his capabilities. In fact, humanities strengths have been so convoluted by this intruder that they actually work against him. Mankind has lived in this impaired condition for so long that they do not even know that there is any other way of life available. Man has been conditioned and conformed to believe that only what he experiences physically is reality, not realizing that his perceptions in the natural blind him from the unseen potential he was originally destined for. How did this happen? What did man fall from? To find these answers we must go to the only book that reveals humanities condition and cure, the Bible. Specifically, the book of Genesis to answer these questions.

*"And God said, "Let us make man in our image, after our likeness. And let them have dominion over the fish of the sea and over the birds of the heavens and over the livestock and over all the earth and over every creeping thing that creeps on the earth."* **Genesis 1:26**

Man's primary function was that of a ruler. He was created in the image and likeness of God to rule and reign over the earth. The Hebrew word for dominion in this verse means to tread down, subjugate and rule. These are the acts of kings! God states later in verse 28 that they were to,

*"Be fruitful and multiply and fill the earth and subdue it, and have dominion..."*

Man was called to subdue, subjugate, bring under dominion the earth realm. That means there were elements and things present that would have to be put under foot. More on this later. Adam, the first man, was given the responsibility over God's creation to *"work it and keep it" (Genesis 2:15)* showing that he was commissioned

2

to not only cultivate the earth but guard it from possible adversaries.

Psalm 8:3 -8 states,

*"When I look at your heavens, the work of your fingers, the moon and the stars, which you have set in place, what is man that you are mindful of him, and the son of man that you care for him? Yet you have made him a little lower than the heavenly beings and crowned him with glory and honor. You have given him dominion over the works of your hands; you have put all things under his feet, all sheep and oxen, and also the beasts of the field, the birds of the heavens, and the fish of the sea, whatever passes along the paths of the sea."*

This Psalm of David reiterates Adam's original position. Another Psalm states:

*"The heavens are the Lord's heavens, but the earth he has given to the children of man"* **Psalm 115:16**

What happened? How did man get to the place where he is today if he was created for so much more?

*"Now the serpent was more crafty than any other beast of the field that the Lord God had made. He said to the woman, "Did*

*God actually say, "You shall not eat of any tree in the garden?" And the woman said to the serpent, "We may eat of the fruit of the trees of the garden, but God said, "You shall not eat of the fruit of the tree that is in the midst of the garden, neither shall you touch it, lest you die." But the serpent said to the woman, "You will not surely die. For God knows that when you eat of it your eyes will be opened and you will be like God, knowing good and evil." So when the woman saw that the tree was good for food, and it was a delight to the eyes and the tree was to be desired to make one wise, she took of its fruit and ate, and she also gave some to her husband who was with her, and he ate." Genesis 3:1-6*

This act of disobedience was more than just partaking of forbidden fruit. It was an act of treason, and the forging of an alliance with rebels who were in opposition to God. Man, through this pact, became one with Satan partaking of his nature, and becoming his son. The authority that Adam had was seized, and humanity was perpetually hijacked to do the will of the oppressor. By becoming one with the nature of Satan, man became an enemy of God. The one with dominion became dominated, the ruler now became the ruled, the king now exiled. The source of Godly rule had departed from Adam, and now he and all of his descendants were sold into slavery.

4

atan himself bears witness to this in his temptation of the Last
dam: Jesus Christ in Luke 4:5,6

*And the devil took him up and showed him all the kingdoms
f the world in a moment of time, and said to him, "To you I
ill give all this authority and their glory, for it has been
elivered to me, and I give it to whom I will."*

otice that Jesus did not argue with this statement. And also notice
at the devil did not claim dominion, but authority.  Being a spirit
ntity, he can only exercise the dominion mandate through flesh,
owever, because of Adam's sin nature he was given authority over
umanity to use them to bring about his will in the earth.

his transfer of man's authority is further illustrated in 2 Corinthians
4 where the Apostle Paul refers to Satan as, *"the god of this
orld."* This title was Adam's original position in the creative order,
ut that designation has now been given to Satan.

is influence is all over the world system.

*We know that we are from God, and the whole world lies in
e power of the evil one."*       *1 John 5:19*

The human predicament is further noted in the Epistle to the Ephesians where the Apostle Paul reminds the church of their onc fallen state.

*"And you were dead in your trespasses and sins in which you once walked following the course of this world, following the prince of the power of the air, the spirit that is now at work in the sons of disobedience—among whom we all once lived in the passion of our flesh, carrying out the desires of the body and the mind and were by nature children of wrath, like the rest of mankind." Ephesians 2:1-3*

Notice these seven things the Apostle Paul states about our sinful condition:

1. We were dead in our trespasses and sins and walke in them
2. We followed after the course of the world system
3. We were followers of the prince of the power of the a
4. We followed the spirit of disobedience
5. We lived in the passions of our flesh
6. Carried out the desires of the body and the mind

7. Were by nature children of wrath, like the rest of the world

Paul again peers into the depraved existence of fallen man in 2 Timothy 2:24-26. In his instruction to Timothy regarding his service to the Lord he admonishes:

*"And the Lord's servant must not be quarrelsome but kind to everyone, able to teach, patiently enduring evil, correcting his opponents with gentleness. God may perhaps grant them repentance leading to a knowledge of the truth, and they may come to their senses and escape from the snare of the devil, after being captured by him to do his will."*

This verse states that when we were under the devil's influence, we were not in our right senses, the Greek denotes someone who is not "sober minded" and has lost "sound senses." The King James Version states that we were in "opposition to ourselves" which means that we were living and thinking contrary to our original design and function. We were not operating in our true identity.

*"Then with meekness you'll be able to carefully enlighten those who argue with you so they can see God's gracious gift of repentance and be brought to the truth. This will cause them*

*to rediscover themselves and escape from the snare of Satan who caught them in his trap so that they would carry out his purposes." 2 Timothy 2:24-26 TPT*

Pay close attention to the phrase *"rediscover themselves."* Is this not what happened to the Prodigal Son in Luke 15:17, *"But when he came to himself..."* ?

 This shows us that man was captured and was doing the will of the devil before redemption was wrought in Christ. These last two scriptures clearly reveal that man went from king to slave. However the enemy has blinded humanity from this reality convincing them that what they see and know is all there is. People have lived "east of Eden" for so long that they have no reference to where they came from, and what is currently available to be restored in Christ Jesus.

In order for Satan to keep his grip on humanity he has devised a system of operations that conceals the truth in plain sight!

# The Great Cover Up

*"And even if our gospel is veiled, it is veiled to those who are perishing. In their case the god of this world has blinded the minds of the unbelievers, to keep them from seeing the light of the gospel of the glory of Christ, who is the image of God."*
*2 Corinthians 4:3,4*

The tactics of the enemy do not change. What he did to us before coming to Christ, he continues doing after we have been introduced to Jesus. His goal, whether we are lost or saved, is to conceal and hide what God has done for us in Christ! Whether through the trappings of our world, or the blinders of religious tradition, he is relentless in his schemes to cover up and camouflage the truth from us!

In fact, the Greek word for "veiled" in this passage means to cover-up, keep secret, cover over and hide. It is the word "Kalupto" in the Greek and it is akin to another Greek word "Kalube" which describes the building of a hut or cabin to hide something. The enemy cannot eliminate truth, but he can cover it up with the facade of distractions, personal goals, desires, and lusts.

Another key word in this verse is "blinded" which is the Greek word "typhloo." This word describes the "darkening of the mind" or "a cloudy, smokey myopia." It is not absolute blindness, but an obscuring that brings about a "blunt mental discernment." In other words, our ability to see is obscured by other things. It is not that these truths are not in plain sight, they are obfuscated by our focus on what the enemy is building in our lives with our full cooperation.

The word "mind" in this text is interesting in that it denotes the "designs of the mind, or mind games" also "systemic understanding." So, this "blinding of the mind" is a total arresting of our understanding, an impairment in how we think, and perceive the things of God. The enemy seeks to distort our understanding of God at the systemic level with mind games and mental tricks that impede clear lucidity.

Notice that Jesus quoted Isaiah 6:9,10 in regard to the disciple's question concerning His use of parables in the public forum. In this passage, He reveals how the Kingdom of God works, or doesn't work, in the lives of people.

*For this people's heart has grown dull, and with their ears they can barely hear, and their eyes they have closed, lest they should see with their eyes and hear with their ears and understand with their hearts and turn and I would heal them."*
*Matthew 13:15*

Notice their heart had grown dull, their ears they can barely hear, and their eyes they have closed. How does this happen?

Jesus further illustrates man's condition in the Parable of the Sower in Mark 4. In describing the effects of the seed of the Word of God in four different soils of the human heart, Jesus stated in verse 18 concerning the soil with thorns,

*"They are those who hear the word, but the cares of the world, the deceitfulness of riches, and the lust of other things enter in and choke the word, and it proves unfruitful."*

The word for care in this verse is "Merimna" which could be properly translated as distraction. The Greek word for world is "Aionos" and means time periods, so we could state that this verse says, "the distraction of our times." The wiles of the devil are unique to your specific season and time! That is why they seem new when they are just the same old tricks.

The blindness used by the enemy is a diversion tactic that places our focus on other things, blinding us to the real things that have the ability to set us free!

Jesus referred to this tactic in Matthew 6:19 -24:

*"Do not lay up for yourselves treasures upon the earth where moth and rust destroy and where thieves break in and steal, but lay up for yourselves treasures in heaven, where neither moth nor rust destroys and where thieves break in and steal. For where your treasure is, there your heart will be also."*

The last statement in this verse in the Greek is a little more pointe In the original language it is stated as, "Wherefore is the treasure you; there will be also the heart of you." Jesus is referring to the number one distraction psychological operation of the enemy and his system which is the accumulation of stuff and money.

*"Do not love the world or the things in the world. If anyone loves the world, the love of the Father is not in him."*
*1 John 2:15*

The use of the word world is relevant to our understanding of thes passages. There are different Greek words that are used for "worl in the New Testament. To properly exegete the scripture we must also acknowledge the context in which the word is used. The word

12

used in this passage is the Greek word "Kosmos" and it means system, order, arrangement, and adorning. So, we could properly translate this as "world system". We are not to love the world system, neither the things that are in the world system. If we love the world system, the love of the Father is not in us! John continues to unveil the composition of this world system in the following verses.

*"For all that is in the world—the desires of the flesh and the desires of the eyes and pride of life—is not from the Father but is from the world." 1 John 2:16*

Now we are getting the idea of what the enemy uses to blind us! The lusts of the flesh, carnal appetites, the lust of the eyes, coveting, envy and pursuit of things, and the pride of life, or as the Greek states "the boasting of life"—gloating and finding great confidence in our achievements and acquisitions. This is where comparison and competition find their roots! But what does he want to blind us from? Remember whether we are saved or lost the objective is the same!

*"In this case the god of this world has blinded the minds of the unbelievers, to keep them from seeing the light of the gospel of the glory of Christ, who is the image of God." 2 Corinthians 4:4*

Dropping down to verse six we can see the full import of the enemy's reason for concealment.

*"For God, who said, "Let light shine out of darkness," has shone in our hearts to give the light of the knowledge of the glory of God in the face of Jesus Christ."     1 Corinthians 4:6*

I think that you should be starting to get the picture that the "face of Jesus Christ" is your true identity! Satan had enough trouble with one of them on the earth, and he certainly does not want others roaming around! More on this later.

Now back to Matthew 6. Jesus is talking about our treasure, the center of our lives, what it's steeped in, what is its focus.

*"For your heart will always pursue what you esteem as your treasure."     Matthew 6:21 TPT "for where you treasure is, there your heart [your wishes, your desires, that on which you life centers] will be also."          Matthew 6:21 Amplified*

Now he gets to the root of the problem in verse 22 which is optics.

*"The eye is the lamp of the body. So, if your eye is healthy, your whole body will be full of light, but if your eye is bad, you whole body will be full of darkness. If then the light in you is darkness, how great is the darkness!"          Matthew 6:22-23*

14

Possessions are not the real problem; it is our perception of them that is the issue which is the pride of life or boasting of life. The Amplified Classic version states,

*"The eye is the lamp of the body. So if your eye is sound your entire body will be filled with light. But if your eye is unsound, your whole body will be full of darkness."*

The Message Bible paraphrases this verse this way:

*"Your eyes are windows into your body. If you open your eyes wide in wonder and belief, your body fills up with light. If you live squinty eyed in greed and distrust, your body is a dank cellar. If you pull the blinders on your windows, what a dark life you will have."*

*"The eyes of your spirit allow revelation-light to enter into your being. If your heart is unclouded, the light floods in! But if your eyes are focused on money, the light cannot penetrate and darkness takes its place. How profound will be the darkness within you if the light of truth cannot enter." TPT*

The Matrix of Satan, which is the world system, continues to enchant, ensnare and entertain humanity into desiring a substitute existence over real life. The propaganda of the wicked one is designed to appeal to the carnal nature of man, and immerses him in the lust of the flesh, eyes and pride of life. A velvet noose, an appearance of comfort, ease and security by the pursuit of things, and personal achievements mask the greater destiny already available to you in Christ!

*"For the love of money is a root of all kinds of evil. It is through this craving that some have wandered away from the faith and pierced themselves with many pangs." 1 Timothy 6:10*

Money was not the cause of their downfall; it was the love of it. Remember Jesus stated,

*"For your heart will always pursue what you esteem as your treasure." Matthew 6:21 TPT*

What you focus on or fix the beams of your eyes on is what you become. This is a vital truth to finding out who you really are. The enemy has an alternative image for you to focus on steeped in the appetites and desires of this world. He works on it even before you take your first breath because it is costly to him if you find out the truth!

So, we see the old bait and switch, the weapon of mass distraction used by the enemy to conspire against humanity. This has been used by conspirators in every human age since the fall of man, diversion to bring about subversion. I hope you are seeing that you have been a pawn in the biggest scandal in history: The Concealing of the Sons of God!

This should be very upsetting to you! Being robbed of your destiny and being deprived of your rightful place in the created order. But I have good news, keep reading!

# Chapter Two: WHO ARE YOU?

**"C'mon tell me who are you?**

**Cause I really wanna know" - Who are you? The Who**

In the late 70's, Pete Townshend of the rock group The Wh set to music probably the most important question facing humanity in any era or generation, who are you?

As we saw in the last chapter, this is the source of the great cover up. Massive amounts of resources have been expended, and the mobilization of armies has been commissioned to either aid or impair the answer to this all-important question. The response to this query is the difference between success or failure, between living as an accident waiting to happen or walking in purpose. You identity defines function, authority and destiny, three things that ar integral to human existence. These components are necessary if we are to live lives of purpose. Without them we are rudder-less, random and accidental in our living, opening us up to chaos and pain.

What if I told you that the face you see in the mirror every morning is not the real you? That although your body is made of earth, the real you is from somewhere else?

Notice Genesis 2:7:

**"then the Lord God formed the man of dust from the ground and breathed into his nostrils the breath of life, and the man became a living creature."**

The Bible is the only book that defines the true make-up of man. The scriptures teach that man is tripartite or three parts. Man, who as we saw in the last chapter was created in the image and likeness of God, can function in three dimensions.

**"Now may the God of peace himself sanctify you completely, and may your whole spirit and soul and body be kept blameless at the coming of our Lord Jesus Christ."     1 Thessalonians 5:23**

You are a spirit being, who has a soul which houses your mind, will and emotions, and you live in a physical body. The Bible identifies the real you as your spirit.

**"So I do not run aimlessly, I do not box as one beating the air. But I discipline my body and keep it under control, lest after**

*preaching to others I myself should be disqualified." 1 Corinthians 9:26,27*

Notice that Paul states, "I discipline my body" and "I keep **it** under control." It is amazing that what we most exclusively identify as ourselves is referred to as an **"it"** in the scriptures. He states that I, the real man, disciplines **it**, the body, and brings **it** into subjection (KJV). So, the real you is not your body!

In 2 Corinthians 4:7, Paul reveals,

*"But we have this treasure in jars of clay, to show that the surpassing power belongs to God and not to us."*

The treasure is your spirit in union with Christ, and the jars of clay refer to your physical body. Jars may have many different shapes and sizes, and some are more physically appealing than others. However, the true treasure is what is in the jar, not the jar itself.

Jars can be deceiving and revealing. Sometimes a beautifully crafted jar can contain a putrid substance, and other times a more modest jar can house the most beautiful, aromatic or delicious ingredient. The old adage, "Never judge a book by its cover" seems applicable, but what is in us is only treasure when Christ dwells in our hearts by faith. This is the treasure that Paul is referring to.

*"The good person out of his good treasure brings forth good, and the evil person out of his evil treasure brings forth evil."* **Matthew 12:35**

Again, Paul records in 1 Corinthians 5:1,

*"For we know that if the tent that is our earthly home is destroyed, we have a building from God, a house not made with hands, eternal in the heavens."*

In regard to the first advent of the Lord Jesus, the Apostle John states that, "the word became flesh and dwelt among us (John 1:14)." Another translation states "the word became "tabernacled" referring to the tent of meeting in the Old Testament. Peter in his 2nd Epistle declared, "since I know that the putting off of my body will be soon," or as the KJV translates, "the putting off of my tabernacle is at hand."

From these passages we see that the body is compared to a tent, this was one of the main types and shadows provided by the Tabernacle of Moses, a tent of skins housing the Shekinah Glory of God.

The world we live in is prone to the superficial and various judgements are made regarding the outward appearance. However, God never operates this way. Remember, this world operates in the lust of the flesh, the lust of the eyes and the pride of life. These hide the truth of what cannot be touched, seen, or experienced physically.

Fallen man believes only what he can perceive with his physical senses as truth. But he was originally created to operate in the body out of the unseen realm of the spirit. Man was created to live from the inside out, but the Fall caused man to live from the outside in. Without the new birth, man is dominated by the physical world around him, but in Christ we can elevate far above the gravitational pull of the physical and operate in the spirit dimension which is limitless!

# Everything is created twice

This truth is integral if you are going to find your true identity. e have established that you are a spirit creation birthed by God. ur physical body is just simply a vehicle that allows you to live in is physical world. It is not you anymore than your clothes are you, your automobile, or your house is you. You just simply dwell in em. One day you will put off the tent, your tabernacle of flesh and ur spirit will be joined to God. However, until that day you must ep your focus on your inner life rather than focusing on your sh.

*hough the outward man perishes, the inward man is newed day by day." 2 Corinthians 4:16 KJV*

is scripture establishes that you have an outer man, which is ur flesh, and an inward man, which is your soul and spirit mprising what the Bible refers to as the heart, meaning the nter of man. Your heart is what you believe with and abides in e dimension of God.

ur outer man has a code known as your DNA, which is the netic code that stems from your parents, and both sets of grandparents. This code determines your size, features and physical capabilities. It is woven into every strand of your body and is your physical identity marker. However, your inner man has only one contributor: God! Woven within your spirit is a codex that houses all of the information and resources to do what God sent you on earth to do. Most people emphasize their genetics and minimize the spiritual codex that is within them. Before you were born again, this spiritual code was hidden from you, because you were alienated from the life of God, but when Christ came into your life your spiritual giftings, capabilities and perimeters came into the light!

*"If then you have been raised with Christ seek the things that are above, where Christ is, seated at the right hand of God. Set your mind on things that are above not on things on the earth. For you have died, and your life is hidden with Christ in God. Colossians 3:1-3*

Because you have been raised with Christ the emphasis of your life should be on things above where Christ is, not on things on the earth that will perish. For you have died, and your life is hidden with Christ in God. The Greek word for hidden is "Krupto" and is where we get the word cryptic. It means to hide, conceal or lay-up, but not hidden from us, hidden for us! The life you are longing to experience is hidden with Christ in God! The New Birth unveils the mystery, and your continuous searching of things above where Christ is will constantly yield revelation of who you truly are!

*For you formed my inward parts; you knitted me together in my mother's womb, I praise you, for I am fearfully and wonderfully made. Wonderful are your works; my soul knows it very well. My frame was not hidden from you, when I was being made in secret, intricately woven in the depths of the earth. Your eyes saw my unformed substance; in your books were written, every one of them, the days that we were formed for me, when as yet there was none of them." Psalm 139:13-16*

We can see from this verse that you were:

1. Formed and knitted together
2. Fearfully and wonderfully made
3. Framed and made in secret
4. Intricately woven
5. Unformed substance
6. Books cataloging your days before you were born

This proves that you were not an accident, but a deliberate creation of God fashioned for a purpose. You were first created in the mind and heart of God and then placed within your earth suit provided by human procreation!

*"For we are his workmanship, created in Christ Jesus for good works, which God prepared beforehand, that we should walk in them." Ephesians 2:20*

*"who saved us and called to a holy calling, not because of our works but because of his own purpose and grace which he gave us in Christ Jesus before the ages began." 2 Timothy 1:9*

God has prepared you beforehand to walk in His good works preordained for you and gives you purpose (directions) and grace (means) to fulfill your call!

Just as Jesus was The Word made flesh you are a word from God to the times and generation that you were brought into. David stated that the days were formed for him in Psalm 139 and yours were too! You may feel like you do not belong in your time period or that you do not fit in with the current of culture. That alienation is normal for those born from above, but from God's end you are at the right place and at the right time!

*"He came to his own, and his own people did not receive him. But to all those who did receive him who believed in his name he gave the right to become children of God, who were born,*

*not of blood nor of the will of the flesh nor of the will of man, but of God." John 1:11-13*

*"Since you have been born again, not of perishable seed but of imperishable through the living and abiding word of God." 1 Peter 1:23*

*"But our citizenship is in heaven," Philippians 3:20*

Who are you? You are a child of God, born of the imperishable word of God and a citizen of heaven now!

*"Beloved we are God's children now, and what we will be has not yet appeared; but we know that when he appears we shall be like him, because we shall see him as he is." 1 John 3:2*

Notice that we are NOW the Sons of God, not in the sweet by and by but NOW! By virtue of the new birth, we are active citizens of the Kingdom of God with the ability to operate in our full citizenship right here and now. Our birth into the Kingdom unites us as one with Jesus and *"as he is, so are we in this world."* (1 John 4:17)

We are one spirit with Him and are the express image of His person on the earth as a member of His body! (1 Corinthians 6:17; Ephesians 1:23; 1 Corinthians 12:27)

However, this leads us to another aspect of our true identity that may not be as appealing.

*"From now on, therefore, we regard no one according to the flesh. Even though we once regarded Christ according to the flesh, we regard him thus no longer. Therefore, if anyone is in Christ, he is a new creation. The old has passed away; behold, the new has come." 2 Corinthians 5:16,17*

In order to take on your true identity you have to disregard the old one. This is the part that proves to be troublesome in our quest for true identity. Ditching our culture, traditions, and even ethnicity for our true identity in Christ can be painful.

*"There is neither Jew nor Greek, there is neither slave nor free, there is no male and female, for you are all one in Christ Jesus." Galatians 3:28*

We have so many self-identifiers from our time on the earth that to discard them seems sacrilegious. But we are to regard no one, even ourselves, after the flesh when we put on Christ as our identity.

Another aspect that can cause friction is that our identity in Christ is in opposition to the world system that we are living and operating

. So, we must arm ourselves with the proper mindset. Peter states his First Epistle,

*But you are a chosen race, a royal priesthood, a holy nation, people for his own possession, that you may proclaim the excellencies of him who called you out of darkness into his marvelous light." 1 Peter 2:9*

here is not a more exciting scripture than the one you just read! owever, Peter follows this statement with a dire warning,

*Beloved, I urge you as sojourners and exiles to abstain from the passions of the flesh, which wage war against your soul." Peter 2:11*

'e should have nothing to do with the world system and our indset is one of a sojourner and exile. We are not to put our roots to this world or be enamored by it. We are *"In the world, but not f the world."* (John 17:16)

he prevailing mental tone of our lives here on earth must be as a:

1. Foreigner – I am not a citizen here
2. Stranger – I do not belong here
3. Sojourner – I am just passing through

4.     Pilgrim – I am passing through on my way to another destination

5.     Alien – I am of another species, not of this world

The war against our soul that leads to a conflicted and compromised inner life is when we yield to the lust of the flesh, the lust of the eyes and the pride of life. Our identity in Christ is so foreign to this world system that it will many times run cross grain its desires. Seeing ourselves in Christ makes us strange to the world, for this is not our home and we are just passing through!

So, now that you know who you are its time to process the plan of God through prayer!

# Chapter Three: The Undiscovered Country

Prayer is the gateway to the undiscovered country of purpose and destiny. It is through this interaction that the realities we spoke of in the last two chapters come alive. Prayer processes the plan of God for your life and puts you in a position of cooperation. Your destiny has to be pursued because there are enemies that want to keep it from coming to pass. Without prayer we fall into their traps and schemes and can go in seasons of aimless routine. This is where Satan uses time as a weapon, siphoning off years of your life by fruitless endeavors and vapid pipe dreams. Prayer is how you can avoid this.

*That the fellowship of thy faith may become effectual by the acknowledging of every good thing which is in you in Christ Jesus." Philemon 6*

Nothing brings out the acknowledgement of the good things in Christ than a vigorous prayer life. However, only scriptural prayers in line with the New Testament are effective in your quest for true identity. Praying from a place of revelation of what the Word of God says that you are is integral. Fortunately, there are prayers fashioned and designed for just this occasion.

Now we are going to be looking at the New Testament prayers of the Apostle Paul found throughout his epistles. These prayers are vital in helping you walk in your new identity in Christ. As Philemon 6 stated, our *"faith grows effectively by the acknowledging of every good thing that is in us in Christ Jesus."* (KJV) But unlike traditional praying, New Creation praying differs from religious petitions in that it is always offered from the basis of a completed work in Christ Jesus. Especially the two prayers in the letter to the Ephesians. The Apostle offers you a revelation in effective prayer, by showing you the proper way of supplication. Many are asking God to do things He has already done in Christ. Paul teaches that you do not pray to get but pray to see what has already been lavished upon you in Christ. There is and will always be a place for petitioning prayer, where you bring your need and desires to him. However, concerning redemptive realities (things purchased through Christ's work on Calvary), the Apostle intercedes for us to have a *"Spirit of wisdom and of revelation in the knowledge of Him, having the eyes of our heart enlightened, that we may KNOW,"*—that is the pursuit, knowledge that makes us free! (John 8:31,32)—The scripture states that **"My people are destroyed from a lack of KNOWLEDGE."** **Hosea 4:6**

Let's take a closer examination of these powerful prayers uttered by the Apostle Paul to the Churches in Ephesus, Philippi and Colossae. I believe we will find them as effectual as when they were first penned, and applicable to your quest. Let's start with Paul's prayers for the Ephesians:

*"I do not cease to give thanks for you, remembering you in my prayers, that the God of our Lord Jesus Christ, the Father of glory, may give you the spirit of wisdom and revelation in the knowledge of him, having the eyes of your hearts enlightened, that you may know what is the hope to which he has called you, what are the riches of his glorious inheritance in the saints, and what is the immeasurable greatness of his power towards us who believe, according to the working of his great might that he worked in Christ when he raised him from the dead and seated him at his right hand in the heavenly places, far above all rule and authority and power and dominion and above every name that is named, not only in this age but also in the one to come. And has put all things under his feet and given him as the head over all things to the church, which is his body, the fullness of him who fills all in all."* Ephesians 1:16-23

As I explained earlier, the most notable difference between religious prayer and New Testament praying is that it is expressed from a foundation of a completed work in Christ. Perhaps most of your praying, up to this point, has been trying to get God to work on your behalf. However, making these prayers personal puts you in a position to speak from an already established reality, and not from a place of trying to coerce or persuade God to do, but to show you what He has already done! When personalized these prayers take you from trying to "get something" to being desirous to "see something," which is what God has already accomplished for you in Christ Jesus!

So, in order to assist you in personalizing these prayers so that you can effectively receive all that God has for you I have compiled some bullet points to help with your understanding.

### Ephesians 1:16-23

1. **"a spirit of wisdom and of revelation"** –you already have the Holy Spirit according to Ephesians 1:13-14, so this is not referring to another spirit, but to a desire, and fervor to know God more.

2. **"in the Knowledge of Him"**—Not just any knowledge, but the knowledge of Jesus Christ. Matthew 11:25-30

3. **"having the eyes of our heart enlightened"**—Your heart has eyes. Your heart is the inner man comprised of both Soul and Spirit (Hebrews 4:12; 1 Thessalonians 5:23). —Your spirit is called "the hidden man of the heart" (1 Peter 3:9) and is perfect and complete (Hebrews 12:23; Colossians 2:10). However, your soul is in a condition of progressive renewal (Romans 12:2; 3 John 2). Jesus referred to this in Matthew 6:22,23 showing the effect that light has upon your condition, as well as darkness which is characterized by ignorance. The Amplified Bible states, "By having the eyes of your heart fully flooded with light,"—Light carries with it the idea of revelation knowledge as the ability to see clearly. The scriptures state that you are "children of the day, not children of the night" denoting that as a New Creation you are "lit" and should not be in the dark. The KJV states, "that the eyes of your UNDERSTANDING be enlightened"—this gives us insight into the collective working of the heart. Understanding is a part of your soul, which also includes the

emotions or sensibilities, and will. The understanding can also refer to the intellect or mind in the scriptures (Ephesians 4:23). Your spirit is already enlightened (1 John 2:20), within is the "mind of Christ" (1 Corinthians 2:16) so the illumination is directed toward your soul, particularly the mind. Bible revelation knowledge is light to the understanding, causing a unification of soul and spirit, thereby releasing power into your natural life changing the way we feel and what we do!

4. **"that you may know what is the hope to which He has called you"**—your calling is found only in Christ! The KJV states, "the hope of His calling," therefore it is His call upon your life, not your own. We are to be extensions of His Body doing His will, His way. Your place in His Body is a Sovereign act that cannot be altered (1 Corinthians 12:18; Romans 11:29).

5. **"what are the riches of His glorious inheritance in the saints"**—Notice that the inheritance is in the saints collectively and

individually. Because you are identified with "The Beloved" you are a joint heir with Christ! God gave Jesus the inheritance and through identification you also have that same inheritance! (Ephesians 1:11-14; Romans 8:15-17; Galatians 4:1-7)

6. **"and what is the immeasurable greatness of His power towards us who believe"**—The Amplified Bible states that this power is "in us and for us!"

1. There are 4 words used for power in the New Testament, and all four are used in this one verse!
2. "greatness of His power (dunamis)"—Inherent Power
3. "according to the working (energeia)"— Outward or Overt     Power
4. "of His great (kratos)"—Ruling Power
5. "of His great might (ischus)"—Endowed Power

7. These powers were displayed in the resurrection of Christ and are the ultimate exhibition of God's power and these powers are working "in us and for us!" Greater is He that is in you that he that is in the world!

8. **"and seated Him (Jesus) at His right hand in the heavenly places, far above all rule and authority and power and dominion..."–** It is not enough to know your calling, your inheritance, and the power at work in you and for you if you do not have the authority to use it. The remainder of the prayer is the exaltation of Christ and the establishment of Him as the Head of the church, but the church is called His Body, thereby revealing that the church is the extension of the risen Christ upon the earth. Therefore, the same elevated position Christ has is also transferred to you! (Ephesians 2:4-7; Matthew 28:18-20; Mark 16:15-19; Matthew 16:19)

*"For this reason I bow my knees before the Father, from whom every family in heaven and on earth is named, that according to the riches of his glory he may grant you to be strengthened with power through his Spirit in your inner being, so that Christ may dwell in your hearts through faith—that you being rooted and grounded in love, may have strength to comprehend with all the saints what is the breadth and length and height and depth, and to know the love of Christ that surpasses knowledge, that you may be filled with all the fullness of God. Now to him who is able to do far more abundantly than all that we ask or think, according to the power at work within us, to him be glory in the church and in Christ Jesus throughout all generations, forever and ever. Amen."*      Ephesians 3:14 -21

The Passion Translation states it this way.

*"And I pray that he would unveil within you the unlimited riches of his glory and favor until supernatural strength floods your innermost being with his divine might and explosive power. Then by constantly using your faith, the life of Christ will be released deep inside you, and the resting place of his love will become the very source and root of your life. Then*

*you will be empowered to discover what every holy one experiences—the great magnitude of the astonishing love of God in all its dimensions." Ephesians 3:16 -18*

When these revelations become a reality to you this translation states that you will be "empowered to discover!" and that is the purpose of this book because our destiny isn't made it is discovered!

Again, here are some bullet points in regard to this dynamic prayer.

**II Ephesians 3:14-21**

1.  **"He may grant you to be strengthened (kratos) with power (dunamis) through His Spirit in your inner being,"—** Again, notice that the power is located in your inner man or heart. A more literal translation states, "strength to rule with His power by the Spirit in your inner man."

2.  **"So that Christ may dwell in your hearts through faith"—**So that Christ may make Himself at home in your heart. Is Christ at

home in you? Does He have access to your sock drawer, your closets, your bedroom, your bank account and your refrigerator?

3.     **"that you, being rooted and grounded in love,"**—This is certainly one of the main issues in the Body of Christ today. Too few have found themselves rooted and grounded in God's love. It is evidenced in our performance and comparison addictions, our continued alchemy of law and grace, and our love of asceticism. (Galatians 3:1-3; Colossians 2:16-23) It is also evidenced by our continuous wrestling with fear (1 John 4:15-18; 2 Timothy 1:7).

4.     **"may have strength to comprehend with all the saints what is the"**: --Or **"Empowered to Discover"** (TPT)

   a.     Breadth or width – Storage Space – meaning all the categories of the Word of God (2 Timothy 3:16-17).
   b.     Length – Time orientation and dispensationalism (2 Peter 1:12).

c.    Height – Your love relationship with God (1 John 4:7-12).

d.    Depth – Your walk and attitude towards humanity (1 John 3:11-18).

5.    **"and to know the love of Christ that surpasses knowledge"**—The love of Christ surpasses human knowledge. This prayer is a lifelong quest!

6.    **"that you may be filled with all the fullness of God"**—The Amplified Bible states "That you may be filled [through all your being unto all the fullness of God [may have the richest measure of the divine Presence, and become a body wholly filled and flooded with God Himself]!

7.    God is able to do exceedingly abundant above all that we can ask or even think, according to the power that is at work in us!

*"And it is my prayer that your love may abound more and more, with knowledge and all discernment, so that you may approve what is excellent, and so be pure and blameless for the day of Christ, filled with the fruit of righteousness that comes through Jesus Christ, to the glory and praise of God."* Philippians 1:9-11

As with the other two prayers here are some bullet points.

### III Philippians 1:9-11

1. **"love may abound more and more,"**— The true sign of spiritual maturity and balance (1 Corinthians 8:1).

2. **"with knowledge and all discernment,"**—The Amplified Bible states "that your love may extend to its fullest development in knowledge and all keen insight [that your love may display itself in greater depth of acquaintance and more comprehensive discernment]."

3. **"So that you may surely learn to sense what is vital, and approve and prize what is excellent and of real value**

[recognizing the highest and the best and distinguishing the moral differences], and that you may be untainted and pure and unerring and blameless [so that with hearts sincere and certain and unsullied, you may approach] the day of Christ [not stumbling nor causing others to stumble]."-AMP

4.      "filled with the fruit of righteousness that comes through Jesus Christ,"—Notice i is "fruit" singular.

*"And so, from the day we heard, we have not ceased to pray for you, asking that you may be filled with the knowledge of his will in all spiritual wisdom and understanding, so as to walk in a manner worthy of the Lord, fully pleasing to him, bearing fruit in every good work and increasing in the knowledge of God. May you be strengthened with all power, according to his glorious might, for all endurance and patienc with joy, giving thanks to the Father, who has qualified you to share in the inheritance of the saints in light. He has delivered us from the domain of darkness and transferred us to the*

*kingdom of his beloved Son, in whom we have redemption, the forgiveness of sins." Colossians 1:9-14*

Colossians is considered an abbreviated twin of the book of Ephesians and some of the revelations are repeated in these prayers. However, the different phraseology lends to more revelation! Again, a bullet point.

### IV Colossians 1:9-14

1. **"may be filled with the knowledge of His will in all spiritual wisdom and understanding, so as to walk in a manner worthy of the Lord, fully pleasing to Him, bearing fruit in every good work and increasing in the knowledge of God. May you be strengthened with all power according to His glorious might, for all endurance and patience with joy,"**— These prayers are in complete congruency with a prophecy concerning the Messiah in Isaiah 11:2-5. This is our inheritance as sons of God!

The perpetual meditation and study of these prayers will have a profound effect upon your life! A greater awareness of what Christ has achieved and has made possible for you will manifest in a personal awakening of Who He is within you!

*"Now unto him who is able to do exceedingly abundantly above all that we ask or think, according to the power that worketh in us, unto him be glory in the church by Christ Jesus throughout all ages, world without end. Amen.  Ephesians 3:20,21*

# Chapter Four: Hid behind he Stuff

*3ehold he hath hidden himself among the stuff." 1 Samuel ):22*

This phrase from the end of verse 22 of 1 Samuel 10 is vealing. In his reluctance to be appointed as King of Israel, Saul des himself so well that God has to reveal to the people where he  He is "hid behind the luggage" one translation states. The KJV ıy "hid behind the stuff."

; we have progressed to this point, I am sure that you can identify th Saul. We all can. Your real identity is hiding behind the stuff, or e baggage of your previous life. The suitcases filled with your mily culture, ethnicity, and other identity markers obscuring who ›u really are, a king! Because you have only known your previous ay of existence, this new life in the Spirit is foreign to you. The ings of God must be acclimated into your life. They are not tuitive to the old man, or the flesh. In fact, to walk in the way of ›ur new identity in Christ many things will be counter-intuitive to

47

what your former manner of life was like and will incite flat out rebellion from your flesh! It takes the revelation of God to reveal these things to you and prayer, as we saw in this last chapter, is th pathway.

So, we must put away "the stuff" that is concealing who you really are, unpacking the baggage that obscures your clear view of who you are in Christ. This is going to hurt!

We touched on this a little at the end of chapter two, but now we are cooking with gas!

So again, what is "the stuff?"

*"Then Jesus told his disciples, "If anyone would come after me, let him deny himself and take up his cross and follow me For whoever would save his life will lose it, but whoever lose his life for my sake will find it." Matthew 16:24,25*

Your life, as it is presently, and has continued for years is "the stu that conceals who you truly are! So, what does Jesus mean by "saving, or losing your life?" Let's take a closer look!

Jesus states in this scripture that if you are to *"desire to come after Him,"*

## 1.    You are to deny yourself.

The Greek word used for "deny" is a strong one. It means to tterly disown, repudiate and disregard. It also means to utterly ɘfuse to recognize or to ignore your life. True identity is revealed ʰhen the old identity is disavowed. As I stated earlier, in 2 ʲorinthians 5:16 that we are *"to regard no one in the flesh,"* that ɪcludes you! Jesus says that you must utterly deny your culture, aditions and ethnicity in this world to be truly identified with Him!

ɪ Luke 14:26, Jesus makes this controversial statement,

*If anyone comes to me and does not hate his own father and ɪother and wife and children and brothers and sisters, yes, ɪ̯en his own life, he cannot be my disciple."*

ɪ Jesus teaching wholesale hatred for all? Absolutely not! The key ɪat unlocks this verse is the Greek word for "hate" which is ɪiseo." It means to love-less or to esteem less. It is a term of ɪiority and preference to love something or someone else less ɪan something or someone else—to renounce one choice in favor f another.

ɪe NASU Bible translates this verse this way.

*"If anyone comes to me, and does not hate ("love less" than the Lord) his own father and mother…"*

The Passion Translation states it this way,

*"When you follow me as my disciple, you must put aside your father, your mother, your wife, your sisters, your brothers; it will even seem as though you hate your own life. This is the price you will pay to be considered one of my followers."*

In other words, your devotion and union with Christ should supersede all other relationships! Your identity with these persons can no longer shroud your true identity in Christ. He must be first in every human relationship! Any compromise in this area can cause serious issues in putting off the old man and putting on the new. This does not mean that you neglect these relationships or that you have no responsibility to function honorably and faithfully. What it does mean is that your relationships are subordinated under Christ and your preference is to follow Him regardless of what your other important relationships think or perceive. This does bring conflict, but it will also bring great freedom!

This scripture out of the 11th Chapter of Hebrews concerning Moses brings more light on this issue.

*"By faith Moses, when he was grown up, refused to be called the son of Pharaoh's daughter, choosing rather to be mistreated with the people of God than to enjoy the fleeting pleasures of sin." Hebrews 11:24*

The word "refused" is the same word variation that Christ used in Matthew 16:24, instead His is more extreme. This Greek word translated "refused" is "araneomai" means to refuse to affirm or to confess or identify with. This picture of Moses is a most accurate portrait of what Christ is stating in Matthew 16:24,25, leaving the identity with one, and preferring, and giving esteem to another identity! Moses refused something in order to receive something greater! As a true disciple of Christ this will be a continuous process as you walk in prophetic seasons with the Lord. For as we stare into the image of Christ we are transformed from *"glory to glory"* into His very image (2 Corinthians 3:18)!

This passage in Hebrews 11 concerning Moses yields up even more treasure by showing you how Moses endured his difficult mission of delivering the children of Israel from a tyrannical king!

*"He considered the reproach of Christ greater wealth than the treasures of Egypt, for he was looking to the reward. By faith he left Egypt, not being afraid of the anger of the king, for he endured as seeing him who is invisible."* **Hebrews 11:26,27**

The first 40 years of Moses' life was identified as a prince of Egypt educated in all of the religion, traditions and customs of that kingdom. He was a part of the royal family, but when God found him on the backside of the desert an exiled prince of Egypt, God's call was so profound that it caused him to consider distinctiveness with Christ, which was reproach to those who raised him, greater wealth than the treasures in Egypt! Notice it states, *"for he was looking to the reward,"*—what was the prize? The reward was Christ! It goes on to say that Moses, *"endured as seeing him who was invisible."* Where your gaze is fixed, and who you focus on is the difference between success and failure in your quest for true identity and purpose!

Moses had to get out from "the stuff" of his old identity in order to become the person he is known as today. He had to turn his back on relationships, and other identity markers of his previous years of ife. This is the path of all those who seek to find true identity and calling in Christ, however, once God reveals Himself to you and what He has in store for you there is not enough riches in the world that compares to it! The whole 11th chapter of Hebrews is filled with examples of people that changed their identity from one state of existence to the another by simply choosing to believe God, and you can too!

## 2. Take up your cross.

our identity has a mission tied to it! But you have to take it up. It is ot always glamorous. That is why Jesus used the cross as a type f our purpose in God. He does not say, "pick up you crown," or ick up your robe" he refers to the cross which can be heavy, umbersome, uncomfortable, awkward and dirty. But oh, the wards of the journey with it, and the destination of it!

ne of the many spiritual paradoxes in your new life is that the fference between freedom and slavery is what you are bound to. you continue to be bound to the old identity you are going to be a ave, but if you are bound to Christ, you are "the Lord's freeman!"

*"Come to me, all who labor and are heavy laden, and I will giv*
*you rest. Take my yoke upon you, and learn from me, for I am*
*gentle and lowly in heart, and you will find rest for your souls*
*For my yoke is easy, and my burden is light." Matthew 11:2*
*30*

Jesus gives rest to your weary soul through "a yoke and a burden
How does He bring you rest this way? The yoke is a farming tool
that makes two animals one. Their combined strength was used ir
the same way heavy equipment is used to plow land, pull up trees
and other tasks where extreme strength is needed. In the setting
of a yoke there was always a lead beast that would guide the less
animal in the way that it should go. So, in this you can see your
identification with Jesus. He is the lead as we are simply to follow
His strength becomes our strength, but His burden also becomes
ours as well. A yoke also, in Jesus' day, was used in reference to
"taking on" a rabbi's teaching.

*"So Jesus said to the Jews who had believed him, "If you*
*abide in my word, you are truly my disciples, and you will*
*know the truth and the truth will set you free." John 8:31,32*

esus again illustrates the profound truth that freedom depends on what you are bound to. By stating that these believers should *continue in the word" (KJV),* which is taking on the yoke of His eachings, they would in turn *"know the truth and the truth would nake them free." (KJV)*

inding yourself to something and freedom do not necessarily go ogether, but by putting on the yoke of the Master, you are ecoming one with Him by word and deed, thereby receiving the eedom that comes from walking with Him! New life in Christ is not burdenless existence, your pursuit can be weighty at times, but our union with Him makes it light!

*For this light momentary affliction is preparing for us an ternal weight of glory beyond all comparison, as we look not t the things that are seen but to the things that are unseen. or the things that are seen are transient, but the things that re unseen are eternal." 2 Corinthians 4:17,18*

No matter where the Master takes you, your mindset should be that it is preparing you for a glory that is *"beyond all comparison."* Like Moses, your focus should be on the unseen, fixed upon *"him who was invisible"* to gain endurance to plow the field before you.

### 3.   Follow Him.

**"And Jesus said to them, "Follow me, and I will make you become fishers of men." Mark 1:17**

By following the Lord, Jesus stated that He would *"make them to become"* something, in this case, a fisher of men. He would later appoint twelve of them as apostles bringing them into another process of transformation.

*"And he went up on a mountain and called to him those whom he desired, and they came to him. And he appointed twelve (whom he also named apostles) so that they might be with him*

*and he might send them out to preach and have authority to cast out demons." Mark 3:13-15*

*"so that they might be with him."*

This will always be the prime directive in your life, if you desire to do anything for God. You may be focused on the doing of ministry, or the fulfilling of destiny, but Jesus prioritized being with Him over being sent out to preach and casting out devils. As my Father in the faith David Emigh said many times "being comes before doing in the Kingdom of God." You need not to look any further than the example of the Master in seeing this truth.

**Jesus is our model for us, and as we will learn later, a model of us.**

**4.    Lose your life for His sake to find your life.**

This is where it gets really sticky. You may be asking yourself how does one lose their life? Is Jesus talking about martyrdom? You can see that there is a deeper meaning here, so what does *"losing your life"* look like from a practical, applicable standpoint. The key to unlocking this is found in the original language. The Greek word used for life is the word "psuche" which can be more properly translated as soul. You are to lose your soul for Christ's sake if you are going to find your true identity. Your soul, as we explained earlier, is a composition of three parts: Mind or Intellect, Will and emotions or sensibilities. Now you may have already thought that some believers you know have already lost their minds, and you may be accurate. However, this is not talking about loss of mental function, but about surrendering your soul to the Lordship of Christ. I am sure that you can deduce that in order to complete this command of Jesus you will have to surrender and submit three very important things that you have relied on your whole life. Which are:


I Think

I Choose

I Feel

These three areas that comprise the soul must be abandoned and replaced with God's thoughts, God's will and God's fruit!

# Chapter Five: Losing your Mind the Bible Way

**I Think**

*"Do not be conformed to this world, but be transformed by the renewal of your mind, that by testing you may discern what is the will of God, what is good and acceptable and perfect."*
**Romans 12:2**

Your mind or intellect has to be renewed so you can discern the will of God for your life. Your personal thought life has to be transformed by the word of God if you are to see the real you in operation. Otherwise, the carnal mind will continue to keep you ensnared by the old man.

*"For those who walk according to the flesh set their minds on the things of the flesh, but those who live according to the*

*pirit set their mind on the things of the Spirit. For to set the mind on the flesh is death, but to set the mind on the Spirit is fe and peace. For the mind that is set on the flesh is hostile to God, for it does not submit to God's law, indeed it cannot. Those who are in the flesh cannot please God." Romans 8:5-8*

The carnal mind is one of the greatest enemies to who you are in Christ. This verse states that if you are mindful of the things of the flesh that death will be the result. But life and peace are the result of a mind set on the things of the spirit.

The Word of God is like a computer operating system, it is the information that powers the hardware of what God has put within you. The Word discovers, designs, and deploys the gifts that God has given you in Christ. The renewed mind is the gateway to the things of the spirit manifesting in your flesh. An unrenewed mind is a major obstacle to seeing what God has done within you and seeing it manifest in the natural world.

His thoughts must become your thoughts so that His ways will become your ways. Your mind, which has been hooked into the matrix of this world system, must be disconnected from and connected to your new life in Christ. This is done through the continuous consumption of the Word of God.

*"And you were dead in trespasses and sins in which you onc walked, following the course of this world, following the princ of the power of the air, the spirit that is now at work in the sons of disobedience—among whom we all once lived in the passions of our flesh, carrying out the desires of the body an the mind, and were by nature children of wrath, like the rest o mankind." Ephesians 2:1-3*

We have looked at this scripture before, but it describes your condition before Christ perfectly. Looking at a few key words in these verses will give us insight into why the renewing of the mind is vital to experiencing your new life in Christ.

The Apostle Paul reveals that you were:

62

*"dead in trespasses and sins"* this is in the locative progressive tense in the original language meaning there was no way out of *"the law of sin and death"* for you! You were on a steady progression of fatality that would eventually end in physical death and eternal separation from God. And that you *"habitually walked following, or according to, the course of this world"* which conveys that you could not help but follow the ideas of your society, and the philosophies of your set times of culture! No matter how much you strove for individuality you were programmed to believe certain things by the cultural matrix around you. You were totally plugged into the *"prince of the power of the air"* his heartbeat was your heartbeat, his ways your ways, his thoughts your thoughts. *"The spirit that is now at work in the sons of disobedience"* that caused you to follow or live *"in the lust of your flesh fulfilling the desires of the flesh and of the MIND."* The Greek word used for "fulfilling" or "lived" means to be creatively energized to live in the desires of the flesh and of the mind!

Here we see the fusing of the mind and the flesh, what is called by the Apostle Paul in Romans 8, "The Carnal Mind." We are prone to think that the carnal mind is a mind set on sex and sensuality, but that is only a small portion of its meaning. The New Testament defines it as Flesh ruled, sense ruled, or body ruled. Paul in writing to the church at Corinth stated,

*"But I brothers, could not address you as spiritual people, but as people of the flesh, as infants in Christ. I fed you with milk and not with solid food, for you were not ready for it."*
*2 Corinthians 3:1,2*

He goes onto address certain behaviors that stem from the carnal mind such as *"envy, strife, and division,"* blatant identifiers of someone who's mind is dominated by the flesh. The sensuous mind is hostile to God and His ways and does not submit to His will!

*"For the mind that is set on the flesh is hostile to God, for it does not submit to God's law, indeed it cannot. Those who are in the flesh cannot please God."* *Romans 8:7,8*

As we stated earlier, the carnal mind, or body ruled mind, is public enemy number one in impeding the discovery of the real you.

bused within it is a labyrinth of appetites, desires, thoughts, philosophies, ideologies, and beliefs that are set in opposition to the truth. This is why the Word of God is so important to us!

Paul reveals its limitations in a later verse in 1 Corinthians 3,

*re you not being merely human?" **1 Corinthians 3:4***

mazing that there is nothing more limiting to you than to be **merely human!"**

, the carnal mind is your kryptonite!

e contrast between a carnal ruled believer and a Spirit ruled liever is further illustrated in ***Galatians 5:16 – 26.***

***But I say, walk by the Spirit, and you will not gratify the desires of the flesh. For the desires of the flesh are against the Spirit, and the desires of the Spirit are against the flesh, for***

*these are opposed to each other, to keep you from doing the things you want to do. But if you are led by the Spirit, you are not under the law. Now the works of the flesh are evident: sexual immorality, impurity, sensuality, idolatry, sorcery, enmity, strife, jealousy, fits of anger, rivalries, dissensions, divisions, envy, drunkenness, orgies, and things like these. I warn you, as I warned you before, that those who do such things will not inherit the kingdom of God. But the fruit of the Spirit is love, joy, peace, patience, kindness, goodness, faithfulness, gentleness, self-control; against such things there is no law. And those who belong to Christ Jesus have crucified the flesh with its passions and desires. If we live by the Spirit, let us also keep in step with the Spirit. Let us not become conceited, provoking one another, envying one another."*

Why is the mind so important? Because it is the seat of understanding the thoroughfare between Knowledge and Wisdom Remember what Jesus said in Matthew 13:15b, *lest they should see with their eyes and hear with their ears (Knowledge) and understand with their hearts (Understanding) and turn (Wisdom), and I would heal them."*

Proverbs 4:7 states,

*"Wisdom is the principal thing; therefore get wisdom: and with all thy getting get understanding." Proverbs 4:7 KJV*

Understanding or insight (in the ESV) is integral to translating knowledge which is simply information of data into proper application (Wisdom) which brings freedom, healing, wholeness and salvation to your life. Mind renewal is not just the accumulation of facts but understanding of application which leads to applied learning which makes you free! (John 8:31,32)

Wisdom is the principal thing because it is what sets us free, but it takes understanding to convert knowledge into wisdom.

How do we accomplish this?

*"This Book of the Law shall not depart from your mouth, but you shall meditate on it day and night, so that you may be careful to do according to all that is written in it. For then you will make your way prosperous, and then you will have good success." Joshua 1:8*

Here we see the three aspects of mind renewal:

**1.     God's Word not departing from your mouth (Knowledge)**

Notice it does not state depart from your eyes. This is penned elsewhere in the scriptures especially Proverbs 4:20-23. However, it is not enough to simply read, but we a to recite and proclaim the Word. Speak the Word of our Go

**2.     Meditating in God's Word day and night (Understanding)**

The Hebrew word for meditate means to ponder, utter and speak to oneself over and over. It brings about the imagery of a cow chewing the cud.

## 3.     So that you may be careful to do (Wisdom)

The whole purpose of the first two exercises is to get you to this point where application is achieved through wisdom!

Again, Jesus stated, *"see with the eyes, hear with the ears"* (Knowledge)

*"understand with their hearts"* (Understanding)

*"turn, and I should heal them"* (Wisdom)

A New Testament companion to this is Ephesians 4:22-24,

*"to put off the old self, which belongs to your former manner of life and is corrupt through deceitful desires, and to be renewed in the spirit of your minds, and to put on the new self, created after the likeness of God in true righteousness and holiness."*

Here we see knowledge in *"putting off the old self."* **Romans 6:11** tells us to *"reckon yourselves dead to sin, but alive unto God"* you cannot accomplish this without first hearing that in Christ you are dead to sin and alive unto God. Knowledge of this alone does not aid you in experiencing this vital truth. The verse moves on to, *"and be renewed in the spirit of your minds,"* this is where knowledge goes through the process of understanding. By keeping the truth of God's Word in your mouth and on your mind, insight and understanding will spring forth giving birth to Wisdom of life changing application, *"and put on the new self, created after the likeness of God.."* True freedom come when we put on the new self, Christ! This is done through the progression of Knowledge, Understanding and Wisdom!

# Chapter Six: So, Tell Me Whatcha Want, What You Really, Really Want!

**Choose**

id I mention that these get tougher? We just showed you how to .ose your mind the Bible way" and if that wasn't enough, now we ave to tackle the will. Nothing can be as hard and unyielding as e human will. We prize our ability to choose, to say yes and to y no, and if we can't do that, we value our ability to be passive gressive and just sit it out.

*Vhat? Know ye not that your body is the temple of the Holy host which is in you, which ye have of God, and ye are not ur own? For ye are bought with a price: therefore glorify*

*God in your body, and in your spirit, which are God's." 1*
*Corinthians 6:19,20 KJV*

*"For if we live, we live to the Lord, and if we die, we die to the*
*Lord. So then, whether we live or whether we die, we are the*
*Lord's." Romans 14:8*

If you are in Christ, you are not your own anymore. This phrase is
met with a lot of confusion, and mixed emotions. In one sense, it
exciting from a redemptive perspective, but practically it can be a
bur in your saddle. Salvation and redemption in Christ have more
facets than just having a ticket to heaven. You have not just been
saved "from something," but "to something," "for something," and
"of something."

**360 Degree Salvation:**

    1.     **Salvation "FROM" Sin, Spiritual Death, and the**
    **domain of Satan = Emancipation**
    2.     **Salvation "TO" New Life in Christ, forgiveness**
    **and liberty = Purpose**

**3. Salvation "FOR" the "prize and high calling of Christ" = Destiny**

**4. Salvation "OF" the Father and the Lord Jesus = Responsibility**

veryone loves being delivered from something but being delivered something is an entirely different story. God just doesn't want to ull you out, but to take you into something as well, and that is here the battle of wills come into play. If the Book of Exodus ghlighted the deliverance of Israel from Egyptian bondage, which a type of your rescue from the world, then the Book of Numbers nowcases the struggles of the people of God while going into what od had already prepared for them. Being saved from bondage rings forth shouts of praise, being delivered to something, and for omething can emit rebellion and obstinance. Your greatest restling matches will be with your will. Jesus wrestled with it, and ou will too. If you do not renew your mind your carnal intellect will ontinue to rebel against the will of God, making it extremely fficult for the life of God to manifest through you.

our self-will will be continually served up to God as you walk in the rocess of transformation. The more your will is in line with God's will determines how much this new life will manifest in you. This is done by faith.

*"I have been crucified with Christ. It is no longer I who live, b Christ who lives in me. And the life I now live in the flesh I liv by faith in the Son of God, who loved me and gave himself fo me." Galatians 2:20*

The Apostle Paul's second prayer in Ephesians 3:16-17 in the Passion Translation reads,

*"And I pray that he would unveil within you the unlimited riches of his glory and favor until supernatural strength flood your innermost being with his divine might and explosive power. Then, by constantly using your faith, the life of Christ will be released deep inside you, and the resting place of his love will become the very source and root of your life."*

Obedience to God in all things is not intuitive. Don't think that it is by natural inclination that you walk in obedience to God. This is where the most intense training (or Treinging) begins! Your flesh has had its way for so long that it protests and rebels against anything contrary to its prior way of existence. Because your flesh is in constant revolt to the will and desires of God it will put you in a position of suffering. No, you are not to suffer sickness, disease, poverty and other things that Jesus has redeemed you from, but you will suffer in bringing the rebellious elements of the body and mind into subjugation, and in striving to do the will of God through opposition by the world system.

Speaking of Jesus, the writer of Hebrews states,

*"Although he was a son, he learned obedience through what he suffered." Hebrews 5:8*

The Doctrine of Suffering is a well-documented but overlooked subject of the Bible.

Jesus walked in direct opposition to the systems of this world, and you will too, if you walk in your identity in Him. The suffering that comes from being set apart will put you at odds with the agendas of others and the adversary's plan. In Him, you are well equipped and fortified, but there is suffering in persecution, being misunderstood, mocked, and ostracized because of the seal of God on your life. Jesus was mocked, you will be too. Jesus was laughed at, and you will be too. Even His own disciples misunderstood Him, you also will be misunderstood. Jesus was hated, and you will be too.

*"If the world hates you, know that it has hated me before it hated you. If you were of the world, the world would love you as its own; but because you are not of the world, but I chose you out of the world, therefore the world hates you." John 15:18,19*

*"A disciple is not above his teacher, nor a servant above his master. It is enough for the disciple to be like his teacher, and the servant like his master. If they have called the master of the house Beelzebul, how much more will they malign those of his household." Matthew 10:24,25*

you will see later, Jesus operated as a man anointed by God cts 10:38) and was subjected to limitations that were not a part of  pre-Bethlehemic Glory.

*nd now, Father, glorify me in your own presence with the ory that I had with you before the world existed." John 17:5*

 was limited in time, space, energy, mobility, access, and many ier limiting factors that humanity clothed Him with. These all vide pressure points of suffering when you are trying to fulfill the  of God. Persecution, as stated earlier, also is a form of fering, *"All who live godly will suffer persecution." (2 nothy 3:12)* And also obedience to the will of God when you do  understand, or do not want to comply can exact a toll on you. ese are heady battles that can only be overcome by walking m out in real time. Jesus experienced them all! I have often ught how Jesus allowed the Roman guards to crucify Him on the ss. The answer is found in His prayer in the Garden of thsemane,

*bba, Father, all things are possible for you. Remove this cup m me. Yet not what I will, but what you will." Mark 14:36*

Jesus could submit to crucifixion on Golgotha because He crucified Himself in Gethsemane.

*"And those who belong to Christ Jesus have crucified the flesh with its passions and desires." Galatians 5:24*

Losing self-will is one of the most arduous tasks. If Christ struggled with it, you will too. The first step of mind renewal is important to this process, as the will sets squarely in the middle of the mind and the emotions. Both the intellect and the sensibilities can pull the trigger of the will. As you well know, there are decisions made from the information of the mind, and or, the emotions. Both are flawed. However, the answer to this dilemma is that one has to be renewed (the mind), and the other (emotions) has to be put under subjection. When this is accomplished, the will is free to choose the will of God in any situation. Let's revisit Romans 12:1,2.

*"I appeal to you therefore, brothers, by the mercies of God, to present your bodies as a living sacrifice, holy and acceptable to God, which is your spiritual worship." Romans 12:1*

You will see in the next chapter that our emotions are closely linked to our bodies and have to be offered up as a "living sacrifice" upon the altar of obedience. That means that your flesh, and its sensibilities must be subordinated to a "living death." Because you are "dead in Christ" your carnal emotions are also put to death daily by offering your body up as a sacrifice to God.

*"Do not be conformed to this world, but be transformed by the renewal of your mind, that by testing you may discern what is the will of God, what is good and acceptable and perfect."*
*Romans 12:2*

You will again notice that the mind has to be transformed which is the Greek word for metamorphosis. Only with a renewed mind, and subordinated emotions will you be able to discern, through testing, what is the will of God. The scripture continues by stating that there are three areas to discern:

1. **The Good –"Agoathos" in the Greek meaning "mere faith."**

**2.** **Acceptable – "Euarestos" meaning "coming to knowledge"**

**3.** **Perfect – "Teleios" meaning "middle of the will of God."**

So, the process of discerning the will of God goes from the broad to narrow, as we traverse through testing from "mere faith" towards "coming to knowledge" to finally "the middle of the will of God." In order to arrive at this destination means that not only is your mind renewed by the word of God, but your emotions are in full submission to the will of God. In other words, reason, the voice of your mind, must be renewed while feelings, the voice of your body, needs to be muzzled, if you want to hear your conscience, which is the voice of your spirit.

The Battle of your will is never an easy proposition, but with our mind renewed and our emotions in check, Godly decisions can be made easier.

Jesus said, "If we lose our life, we will find life." If we lose our soul (mind, will, and emotions), we will find our true life!

# Chapter Seven: Sense and Sensibilities

**I Feel**

Continuing on to the third part of the soul, the emotions or sensibilities. I hope that you are gaining an understanding that the "Life" you are to "lose" is the soul that is entwined to this current world system. Each of the components of the soul, which are the mind, will and emotions, were hard-wired to the "course of this world" (Ephesians 2:1,2) before you came to Christ.

*"Do not love the world or the things in the world. If anyone loves the world, the love of the Father is not in him. For all that is in the world—the desires of the flesh and the desires of the eyes and pride of life—is not from the Father but is from the world." 1 John 2:15,16*

Before answering the call of Jesus, your soul was interfaced to what I call the "building blocks" of the world system, the desires of the flesh, the desires of the eyes, and the pride of life. Your carnal mind was united to these three machineries creating a mirage of freedom, but in reality, shackles of slavery. All three parts of the soul (mind, will, and emotions) were stitched into these three elements. The mind or intellect was locked into the data of the lust of the flesh being fastened by the five physical senses. The emotions cohabitated with lust of the eyes by what it perceived "of and in" its physical surroundings. The lust of the eyes ascribes meaning to persons, places and things. And the will was married to the pride of life which brought identity by promoting self-awareness in concert with its surroundings. The pride of life can be translated from the original text as meaning, "the boasting of life." This denotes how you identify yourself, your accomplishments, standing and status in the world scheme. It is your projected self-image that has been groomed over the course of your human experience. Both success and failure can foster pride of life because conceit is not confined to just attainment. Some of the most arrogant people manifest their pride through victimization and fatalism.

Every decision made was in alignment with your perceived self-awareness energized by the lust of the flesh, the lust of the eyes and the pride of life. By identifying yourself with the world system

You were thrust into the "hamster wheel" of a course of life you were never destined by God to live!

*"All the toil of man is for his mouth, yet his appetite is not satisfied." Ecclesiastes 6:7*

Fallen man's appetites for consumption and boasting are insatiable! In a preceding verse Solomon states,

*"Then I saw that all toil and all skill in work come from a man's envy of his neighbor. This also is vanity and a striving after wind." Ecclesiastes 4:4*

Our soul interconnected with the world system brings forth wrong motivations and a faulty foundation for life. The pride of life fosters competition and comparison which manifests as high accomplishment and workaholism. This will drive you to an early grave. That is why we need to get out from "behind the stuff."

This trio of terror's goal is the total bombardment of the senses extrinsically and intrinsically. A total captivity with shackles withou but even worse, fetters within! Now you see why you need to "los it!"

Decisions are triggered by these three elements. As stated earlie the will can be sparked by the logic of the mind, or the feelings of the emotions. The carnal mind thrives in the lust of the flesh, lust the eyes, and the pride of life. They are its lone receiver of information and evidence. Making the natural life a limited existence with no cognizance of spiritual things.

*"The natural person does not accept the things of the Spirit God, for they are folly to him, and he is not able to understar them because they are spiritually discerned.' 1 Corinthians 2:14*

In this passage of scriptures in 1 Corinthians 2 we are introduced two types of existences. The *"psychikos"* man and the *"pnuematikos"* man. Which is just a fancy way of stating the difference between the natural or soulish man and the spiritual man.

*"The spiritual person judges all things, but is himself to be judged by no one."* **1 Corinthians 2:15**

The natural man is plugged into the system, the spiritual man is free from the system!

The emotions are manipulated by this trio as well. Before Christ, how you felt about yourself was limited to these three gateways which are inconsistent and unstable. So, now I believe that you can see that "losing your life (soul)" as Jesus stated is a forsaking of your old identity which was seeded, cultivated and brought to fruition by the Lust of the flesh, the lust of the eyes, and the pride of life. Before Christ, your identity was in these things, the outward and inward lusts, appetites and paradigms that deceived you into thinking that this is all there is. However, many believers still struggle with this last area of "losing your life" which is the emotional realm or sensibilities.

Since your emotions are closely linked with your flesh the power to feel can be incredibly exhilarating or incredibly debilitating. The difference is a renewed mind, an iron will, and subordinated emotions.

As you read the title of this chapter, "Sense and Sensibilities" I am sure that you were confronted with the fact that this literary play or words shows that these two don't usually walk hand in hand. Emotions in motion can mean the absence of sense! One of the main tactics of the enemy is to limit your life by making you a slave to your feelings. People with a low emotional quotient do not usually go very far in life. Their perception of themselves and other is honed from how they feel causing a roller coaster ride for all involved. Roller coasters are fun for a short period of time. I doubt very seriously that anyone would want to live on one, but many do because their emotions are not brought into subjection. Unchecked emotions can hinder relationships, opportunities and from hearing the voice of God!

Emotion can lower your IQ dramatically. Have you ever said something out of anger that forever altered a relationship? Has despair deprived you of an opportunity? Or has levity ruined a significant moment in your life? When driven by emotions we can become a dangerous driver capable of an accident at any moment. Again, visit Jesus' story of "The Prodigal Son," which we alluded to in Chapter One, who asked for his inheritance early, probably an emotional decision, and squandered it on riotous living. When his decisions brought him to one of the lowest places a Jewish man could find himself, a pig pen, the master states,

*"But when he came to himself..." Luke 15:17*

So apparently during this season of his life, however long that was, he was not himself. Emotions fueled by misinformation can lead you to actions, attitudes and decisions that are not in alignment with who you are. Sensibilities can weave a spell that can cause alterations in your thought processes and even assault your core beliefs and values. There is great vulnerability when one has emotions in motion. Without the stabilizing force of the Word of God you can find yourself easy prey for the enemy!

Notice again this passage from 2 Timothy,

*"And the Lord's servant must not be quarrelsome but kind to everyone, able to teach, patiently enduring evil, correcting his*

*opponents with gentleness. God may perhaps grant them repentance leading to a knowledge of the truth, and they may come to their senses and escape from the snare of the devil, after being captured by him to do his will." 2 Timothy 2:24-26*

As we saw in Chapter One the King James version of this verse states two characteristics of the described subject:

1. **"who oppose themselves"**
2. **"that they may recover themselves"**

People under the sway of emotion can be captured by the devil to do his will. There is no greater example that comes to mind than the emotional dynamo of personal offense! Notice the KJV states that "they oppose themselves" that is certainly true of someone that fights off the truth of the Gospel, but also one that fights off the truth of God's word in any situation. Notice also that they have to "recover themselves" so, it is a personal decision on their part, repentance that causes them to escape the snare of the enemy. How? Through repentance, which is by definition "a change of mind" they come to their senses and break out of the emotional cocoon the enemy has swallowed them up in!

The power to feel is more closely allied with the flesh than the other components that make up the soul meaning they are far more likely to react, respond and rehearse what the unbridled flesh would desire to do. Your emotions must be treated just like you were taught about your flesh in the previous chapters. They must be put under subjection to the real you, your spirit!

Let's revisit this scripture,

*But I discipline my body and keep it under control, lest after preaching to others I myself should be a castaway." 1 Corinthians 9:27*

Since feelings are the voice of the body, the whine of the flesh must be treated with the same attitude that the desires and needs of the body are treated with, discipline and subjugation. That means that when emotions are vying for an audience or demand your attention you must subordinate them to the truth of God's word. When you put them under the microscope of the word and scrutinize their basis and motivation through the truth of scripture new responses come forth.

Not all emotions are bad, they are God given and are even attributed throughout the Bible as characteristics of Him. However we must not be mastered by them in that it overrides our relationship and obedience to God.

Being emotionally undisciplined opens you up for deception, manipulation and the snares of the devil. Lose it!

# Chapter Eight: Lifestyle of the New Creation

*He is the beginning...*" **Colossians 1:18**

*Therefore, if anyone is in Christ, he is a new creation. The old
is passed away; behold, the new has come."* **2 Corinthians
17**

Jesus is not just an example for us, but of us. Jesus modeled the
new creation life throughout His earthly ministry. There is no higher
standard of operation than Jesus. As the Son of Man, Jesus
exhibited what a New Creation life should look like. His ministry is
our standard. He was a man anointed by the Spirit of God operating
under the authority of the Father.

*"How God anointed Jesus of Nazareth with the Holy Ghost and power who went about doing good and healing all who were oppressed by the devil for God was with him."* **Acts 10:38**

As Colossians 1:18 states, *"He is the beginning"* the beginning of something new. We know that Jesus as God was and is the beginning.

*"In the beginning was the Word, and the Word was with God, and the Word was God."* **John 1:1**

However, this beginning listed in Colossians is the birth of a new species of being, the New Creation.

*"Yet look at you now! Everything is new! Although you were once distant and far away from God, now you have been brought delightfully close to him through the sacred blood of Jesus—you have actually been united to Christ! Our reconciling "Peace" is Jesus! He has made Jew and non-Jew one in Christ. By dying as our sacrifice, he has broken down*

every wall of prejudice that separated us and has now made us equal through our union with Christ. Ethnic hatred has been dissolved by the crucifixion of his precious body on the cross. The legal code that stood condemning every one of us has now been repealed by his command. His triune essence has made peace between us by starting over—forming one new race of humanity, Jews and non-Jews fused together! Two have now become one, and we live restored to God and reconciled in the body of Christ. Through his crucifixion, hatred died. For the Messiah has come to preach this sweet message of peace to you, the ones who were distant, and to those who are near. And now, because we are united to Christ, we both have equal and direct access in the realm of the Holy Spirit to come before the Father! So, you are not foreigners or guests, but rather you are the children of the city of the holy ones, with all the rights as family members of the household of God." Ephesians 2:13-19 TPT

"For as in Adam all die, so also in Christ shall all be made alive." 1 Corinthians 15:22

We have been made alive for one reason and that is not just to have Heaven as our destination. Many see salvation as just a rescue or a redemption and thank God it is both of those and more! But the real reason for the new creation is the replication of Jesus in His body on the earth!

*"Therefore, as you have received Christ Jesus the Lord, so walk in him, rooted and built up in him and established in the faith, just as you were taught, abounding in thanksgiving. Colossians 2:6,7 ESV*

In his Epistle to the Ephesians, the Apostle Paul declares that the church is *"his body the fullness of him..." Ephesians 1:23 ESV*

Colossians 1:18 states about Jesus, *"He is the beginning...".* This refers to Him as the beginning of a new species of being, a new creation nation with Him being the *"firstborn among the dead."*

sus cleansed us and washed us with His blood, not to just forgive
for our sins and give us Heaven when we die, but so that He
uld make His home inside of us and reign within us!

*anyone loves me, he will keep my word, and my Father will*
*e him, and we will come to him and make our home with*
*n." John 14:23 ESV*

u are now the special dwelling place of God on the earth! He
s and abides in you! This is why Jesus stated to the Apostles in
n 16:7

*evertheless, I tell you the truth: it is to your advantage that I*
*away, for if I do not go away, the Helper will not come to*
*u."*

sus living His life through you by the Holy Spirit is the life you
re created to live. Jesus walked the earth as an example of us.
*"emptied himself"* of His Divine attributes and became a man,
Last Adam, so He could model the New Creation life that you

were called to live. Granted He has the *"Spirit without measure"* and you have the Spirit in a measure, but His life and ministry is t primer for your new life.

*"Truly, truly, I say to you, whoever believes in me will also d* *the works that I do, and greater works than these will he do,* *because I am going to the Father."  John 14:12 ESV*

Now that you have gotten out from "among the stuff" it is time to "walk in Him" which is your identity in Christ. Jesus is the pattern we must follow if you are going to find the real you!

Jesus exampled for us these Six principles of New Creation Livin If you will follow them, you will be successful in fulfilling the will of God for your life.

### 1.    He came not to do His own will -John 6:38
This is key to having the operation of God working in you and through you. Too many have their own plans and wha they think their lives should look like, but only God's will is

96

prepackaged with His Power, Provision and Blessing. The primary focus of Jesus' ministry was the will of God this kept Him from distraction and caused Him to resist temptation.

## 2. His teaching was not His, but The Fathers -John 7:16

During Jesus' earthly ministry the land of Israel was filled with Wisdom teachers and even those that claimed they were the Messiah. One of the differences that I believe stands out is that Jesus never took credit for the teaching that He brought forth. He always gave credit and glory to the Father. It is easy to get **"puffed up"** when revelation comes to our heart, or a truth of God's word becomes real to us. Jesus never fell for this He realized that He could have nothing unless the Father granted it to Him.

## 3. The Father in Him did the works -John 14:10

Just like the last point, Jesus never took credit for one miracle or deliverance that happened in His ministry. He did not allow the manifestations of healing power and signs and wonders to make him conceited, arrogant or lift Him up in pride. He always gave credit to the Father.

**4.      He only spoke what He heard from the Father -
John 8:38; 12:49**

Jesus waited on direction from God and only spoke what He
heard the Father say. His words were powerful because they
were measured and steeped in the mind of God. His words
were always powerful because of this as well.

**5.      He only did what He saw the Father do -John 5:19**

Jesus didn't move unless He saw God move. This requires
patience and self-control if you are to replicate this trait.
Many times, we will fly into a situation without hearing from
God and it creates an even bigger mess! Jesus never did
this. When His good friend Lazarus had been sick and died,
Jesus waited until He was directed by God to go to Bethany
Jesus was never driven by the needs of people; He was
devoted to the will of His Father.

**6.      He was dependent on the Holy Spirit -Matthew
3:16; Luke 4:14 – 19; Acts 10:38**

As stated in the referenced verses, Jesus was fully God and
fully man, however His earthly ministry was done as a man
anointed by the Spirit of God, under the direction of the
Father. Jesus was dependent on the Spirit as you and I are

now dependent on the Spirit. Jesus operated as we are to operate today, and this is how you will replicate His works in your generation.

This is the lifestyle of a New Creation. I am sure that you can see that you had to get out from "among the stuff" so that you could operate in its' realities. These six attributes of Jesus' ministry on earth are counter intuitive and clash head on with the world's ways of being and doing. The world seeks credit, acknowledgement, and use their gifts to gain influence and notoriety. Jesus would have none of that and if you want to live His life through you in proficiency, you will have none of it as well.

I think you will find that Jesus' modeled ministry is in short supply in our culture today. I hope this book spurs you to desire to see it more by taking up the mantle yourself. When the real Jesus is lifted up in our lives, then men will be drawn to Him, but when ministry does not mirror these six attributes the real face of Jesus is obscured. Let's seek to uncover the great coverup and reproduce the real Jesus who lives on the inside of us!

As Senior Pastor of Lake Church Mannford, Oklahoma, Pastor Greg has heart to communicate the gospel in a creative way. In 2007 he began ke Church with a vision to make disciples and to raise and develop aders for the local church. Pastor Greg provides leadership and idance by mixing bold presentation, innovative teaching, and mpassion. Pastor Greg brings fresh revelation by using today's diverse lture, his sharp wit, and jocose expressions, making God's word evant for all. Pastor Greg is a visionary and is passionate about aching the world for Christ.

Pastor Greg has been married to his wife Karen Hurd for 35 years. ey have four sons, 6 grandchildren and currently reside in Mannford,

Look for the next book in the Treign series, **Awaken the Kings**, soon to be released.

Treign is a series of books written by Pastor Greg V. Hurd as part of the core curriculum in the Treign Bible College at Lake Church in Mannford, OK.

Pastor Greg's sermons are available to watch at lake-church.com. Weekly services are streamed live from the Lake Church facebook page and also on the Lake Church icampus page at https://icampus.lake-church.com/.

Made in the USA
Coppell, TX
21 September 2021